Dyspraxia

The SEN series

Dyspraxia

Geoff Brookes

continuum
LONDON • NEW YORK

Continuum International Publishing Group
The Tower Building
11 York Road
London
SE1 7NX

15 East 26th Street
New York, NY 10010

www.continuumbooks.com

© Geoff Brookes 2005

British Library Cataloguing-in-Publication Data
A catalogue record for this book is available from the British Library.

ISBN: 08264 7581 7 (paperback)

Typeset by Servis Filmsetting Ltd, Manchester
Printed and bound in Great Britain by MPG Books Ltd, Bodmin, Cornwall

Contents

Foreword

Dyspraxia is such a frustrating condition. It has few physical manifestations but it has the capacity to determine the shape of someone's life. Yet because it cannot be seen, some find it hard to believe in. They say it is made up, an invention to explain away under-achievement.

Live with a dyspraxic though and you will soon change your mind. You will see a child desperately trying to clutch at life through a veil of fog, always finding that the world is moving faster than they are; always finding that the things they want are, tantalizingly, just out of reach. Oh yes, dyspraxia is real enough and terribly frustrating for everyone who comes into contact with it, whether at home or at school.

This book is only an introduction to a complex condition. There is so much more to say. All I can do is give you a flavour of what it is like and to direct teachers to practical advice that might be of real benefit to dyspraxic children. It is no more than they deserve.

Lastly I should like to dedicate this book to my son David who has dyspraxia. Without him I couldn't have written a thing.

Introduction

Dyspraxic children are lazy
Dyspraxic children are stupid
Dyspraxic children just need to work harder
Dyspraxic children are naughty and disruptive
Dyspraxic children are created by bad parenting
Dyspraxic children will eventually grow out of it

All these statements are wrong.

They are myths but persistent ones and reflect the reluctance of some people to accept the reality of the condition. It has been seen as an excuse for poor behaviour and for inadequate family circumstances. A posh excuse from middle-class parents looking for excuses why their child is letting them down. Thankfully those days are passing. The condition is a real one, with a history and certainly with a future.

Dyspraxia has been called many things in its time. It is probably more accurately described as Developmental Coordination Difficulty but for the purposes of this book I shall use the term dyspraxia. It refers to the way in which the brain works in a different and less precise way for some people than it does for others. And no one knows why this should be.

As knowledge about the brain and how messages

1

are carried within it grows, so does our understanding of what happens when things go wrong. It is impossible to define what is normal within something as rich and complex as the brain, but certainly the dyspraxic child has identifiable difficulties that the rest of us would not want to share. There are symptoms, there are problems, there are frustrations, there are tears.

But there are strategies that can lead to positive outcomes. And while it is important to understand where it comes from, providing support and guidance is what this book is all about. It attempts to ensure that teachers are informed about the condition and, more importantly, enable them to acquire the strategies to provide effective help to the dyspraxic children in their care.

1

What is Dyspraxia?

Developmental dyspraxia is a neurologically based disorder which means it happens within the brain where we can't see it. It is a motor planning difficulty that is present from birth.

What appears to happen is that parts of the motor cortex in the brain don't develop properly. This prevents messages from being transmitted efficiently to the body. So dyspraxics have difficulty in planning movement to achieve a predetermined idea or purpose. Basically, the dyspraxic child cannot make their body do what they want it to do. This must be extremely frustrating.

Technically speaking it is a disorder of these three processes.

1 Ideation – forming the idea of using a known movement to achieve a planned purpose.

2 Motor planning – planning the action needed to achieve this idea.

3 Execution – carrying out the planned movement.

Here are examples of three types of dyspraxia that might make this clear.

Oral Dyspraxia

This causes the child to be unable to reproduce mouth movements. So if they were asked to put their tongue in their cheek they would be unable to carry out the instruction, even though they would be able to do it unconsciously.

Verbal dyspraxia

A child will have difficulty in making sounds or in forming words out of sounds. So when trying to say 'ship' they might say 'bip' no matter how hard they try. There is an immaturity of the speech production area of the brain.

Motor dyspraxia

This prevents a child moving in a planned way. They know that they want to catch a ball but they cannot organize the necessary movements to achieve this.

What is important is a recognition that it may affect any or all areas of development – sensory, physical, intellectual, emotional, social or language. And this lack of efficiency in delivering and receiving messages can happen in any of the millions of connections within the brain. Every person is different as a result. And every dyspraxic is different too.

2

The Science

If we understand the science then we will understand the origins of the condition. It is important that we have a basic understanding of how the brain works in normal circumstances so that we can see where the problems might be when things deviate from that norm. We will see how the dyspraxic child is the victim of things over which they have no control at all, for the origins of the condition lie at the earliest stages of brain tissue development in the womb.

Our brains are made up of neurons that are connected by nerve fibres or axons to their various destinations in the body. They are arranged in lobes in those familiar two halves or hemispheres.

- ♦ Each hemisphere is also divided into lobes – the Frontal, Parietal, Temporal, and Occipital lobes.
- ♦ The Limbic System is, among other things, the emotional centre of the brain.
- ♦ Different functions of the body are controlled by different parts of the brain.
- ♦ 'Messages' and information travel along nerve fibres by way of the Spinal Cord, Cortex, Cerebellum and the Corpus Callosum.

Dyspraxia

♦ Incoming information from the senses – touch, taste, sight, smell, hearing, movement, balance, warmth, language, experience, sense of self – is organized and stored in the brain, to be retrieved for use as it is needed.

It is not a surprise that minor disruption to something so complex can have far-reaching consequences. This disruption, which can cause dyspraxia among other things, can happen as the brain develops in the womb, though no causes for such problems have yet been identified.

The pre-birth growth of a baby goes through clearly defined developmental stages. From the moment of conception the fertilized egg divides and multiplies. Some cells will separate from the rest and continue to multiply at their own increased rate to become the nerve cells (neurons) of the brain. After six months gestation the neurons, with their axons, have been produced and subsequently no further new neurons are grown. Furthermore, they do not regenerate. This is an important point. A neuron that is damaged or dies, or does not complete its growth and thus reach its destination, will not be replaced or renewed, unlike cells in other parts of the body. Thus, if a cell or group of cells fails to complete its growth and reach its destination, future sensory information from that area will be impaired. A route will not be established; a connection will not be formed. This idea of connections not quite reaching the right destination is a crucial point in understanding dyspraxia. This system failure can happen in any part of the brain, whether that part deals with movement, speech, emotion. Hence the wide-ranging nature of dyspraxia.

A development that does continue, and indeed does so until old age, is that of the individual cells. They grow dendrites and form connections within the brain. There are billions of neurons in every brain, each with many connections with other cells. For correct operation, neurons have to develop in sufficient numbers in the right areas of the brain and they must extend to the correct destination. This has to be achieved by the appropriate developmental stage or it will never occur at all.

There are two kinds of neurons – those carrying messages to the brain (sensory) and those carrying messages from the brain (motor). The implications of inappropriate development in either direction are obvious and suggest the ways in which messages can be disrupted.

After six months gestation the axons begin to develop an insulating fatty sheath called myelin. This is important because it allows messages to be carried efficiently along them. The best analogy is that it functions rather like the insulation around an electric wire. Without it the messages or impulses would fly around everywhere. The myelin makes sure that the messages are concentrated and heading for the correct destination. It takes time for this protective sheath to be completed. It is in place by around three months of age; babies younger than that will make random reactive movements, without purposeful intent. After myelination, movements will slowly become more deliberate, with a purpose and intent. The eyes may become more focused, and the baby may recognize or touch a face and smile.

The successful creation of such secure message paths is a vital part of our development. It is interesting to note that multiple sclerosis is a direct result of a partial breakdown of the myelin sheath and message-carrying capacity.

The connections between nerve cells, dendrites and synapses continue to increase throughout a lifetime; their growth stimulated by the demands of the environment, by relationships, experience and as learning takes place. The brain is involved in a huge amount of traffic every day and if messages, like trains, can't get through straight away then they have to be re-routed. Hence delays and disruption when there are neurological leaves on the line.

Indeed the idea of a railway network is perhaps a good way of getting hold of the concept of dyspraxia and may prove a useful comparison to share with a dyspraxic child who is anxiously trying to understand what is happening to them. There are all these messages whizzing round the brain on special tracks and sometimes there is something blocking the line. So the message goes the long way round. It needs to find a different way into the station.

Praxis

The term 'dyspraxia' comes from the Greek word 'praxis' which means, doing, acting, deed or practice. Praxis is a central thing about us as beings. It links what goes on in our heads with what we actually do. It enables us to function in our world. So we can dress, eat with cutlery, write, catch a ball, swim. These are not instinctive actions. They are things that we plan to do. We don't make a cup of tea at an instinctive level. We think through a series of actions. Most animals don't have a great deal of praxis. It is one of the things that makes us different.

Praxis develops as connections are refined in the brain. As we grow, we carry out actions of increasingly better quality, allowing us to do things that are more complicated. Look at a baby. They begin by making largely uncontrolled movements, waving arms and legs around without much of a purpose. Soon these actions are controlled by the will and carried out with premeditated purpose – to touch a rattle, to look at mother. This involves some motor planning, some praxis. These actions are not random or accidental. The child is recalling previous actions and repeating them, modelling what it does now on what it successfully achieved before. Actions soon become more complicated as the brain acquires more retrievable memory of movement sequences.

Learning to talk requires us to organize a specific combination of muscles to produce the right controlled collection of sounds in the right sequence at the appropriate time to achieve a planned purpose. This is praxis – and this is the source of the problem for dyspraxics.

So what goes wrong?

Let's go back to the three processes involved in carrying out an action, because if we look at how an action happens, we can see where it goes wrong for the child with dyspraxia.

Ideation

If a child comes across some wooden blocks for the first time they must gather as much information about them as possible. What shape are they? How do they feel? What do they taste like? How do they behave? Are they stable or mobile? That information has to be collected, arranged and stored. Then, when required, it can be retrieved and the knowledge of that experience can be used to form the idea of building something with the bricks. For this you need a plan of action.

Motor Planning

This happens in the parietal lobe of the brain. When it receives the idea, the Planning Department has to work out and plan the instruction it has received. Which part of the body should be where, which particular muscles should contract or relax, in what sequence and by how much. It needs to remember the past experience that was gathered about these blocks. This will refine the instructions it is about to send out – the weight of the blocks, the size – and determine the sequence in which the muscles are to work. Then it is time to send out the messages for action.

Execution

Muscles can only either contract or relax in response to messages received from the brain telling it what to do, for how long and in what order. Messages then travel back from the muscle to the brain so that the action can be monitored and revised.

When you see the process broken down in this way then it is a wonder anything ever happens at all. Described in this way it seems so complex. The simple act of stirring a cup of tea seems impossible. If there were sand at the bottom of the cup then the muscles in your hand would flash a message back to the Planning Department and, if they are not out to lunch, they will work out what is going on by comparing this experience with a previous one. 'Something feels wrong. It is not like it was when I stirred before. It is not dissolving like sugar . . .' and so on. Information is flying backwards and forwards all the time as the situation is assessed.

The three stages are interdependent and they rely for the success of any action upon the messages travelling on the correct tracks and making the correct connections. If anything interrupts the messages or if the Planning Department is indeed out to lunch and the brain can't recall doing this action before quickly enough, then the process will be disrupted. And that is what dyspraxia does for you.

What does all this mean?

In all this complexity of information gathering and delivery something is going wrong. The messages are not getting through or are not producing the right results. Who knows what is happening? Perhaps the information was not collected or transmitted or stored properly. Perhaps it was stored in the wrong place. Perhaps it was taken out and then put back in the wrong place. Perhaps the Planning Department didn't send the messages to the right place. Perhaps the right nerve fibres are missing or are incomplete. Whatever is happening the praxis is failing. So the child may not be able to pick up the bat quickly enough to hit the ball, or may not be able to work out how to move from chewing to swallowing. This is also why it can be such an inconsistent condition. Yesterday the messages were getting through, the information was retrieved and the task completed. They could colour in the clown without straying outside the lines. Today the plan has been lost. The filing system broke down. It was put back in the wrong place. They can't colour in the clown. Of course the file may turn up again tomorrow. Or the child may have to relearn the skill.

Colouring in is a simple example, but there could be a system malfunction at any location in the brain. Just imagine how complicated things can become if there is a problem in the area that sorts out relationships and emotions.

3
Questions

Is dyspraxia new?

Of course not. It has always been there for as long as the brain has been operating. It is obvious really. The brain is such a complex organ it can't be a surprise if parts of it are wired up differently. It is those brain connections that make us individuals. Why is one person good at tennis and their brother absolutely useless? Why is handwriting so unique? How did Shakespeare write as he did? Why do some ideas leap into your mind from nowhere?

All our brains work differently and they process all our different experiences, seeing insights, forming connections. And if one part of the brain isn't talking successfully to another then things are bound to be unpredictable.

Developmental dyspraxia was finally categorized by doctors in the twentieth century. It was originally described as 'congenital maladroitness'. In 1937 Dr Samuel Orton described it as 'one of the six most common developmental disorders, showing distinctive impairment of praxis'. Jean Ayres called it 'a disorder of sensory integration' in 1972. In 1975 Dr Sasson Gubbay called it 'Clumsy child syndrome'.

Dyspraxia

It has been called other things too. Developmental awkwardness. Sensorimotor dysfunction. Developmental coordination disorder. Today, the World Health Organization lists it as the 'Specific Developmental Disorder of Motor Function'. Lots of names, but what are far more important than a label, are the help and understanding a child receives from those around them.

What are the symptoms?

It doesn't have a common set of symptoms, so it is not what doctors call a unitary disorder like scarlet fever or mumps, where everyone suffers in the same way. Each person is affected in different ways and to different degrees.

The fact that each child is affected in different ways is hardly a surprise, given the complexity of the brain and its workings. Naturally, in the majority of cases, parents notice it first. Developmental stages may not be reached or negotiated. The child may be late in learning to sit or stand or walk. As far as crawling is concerned, some dyspraxic children never manage it at all. Expected skills may not be mastered. An early indication may be feeding difficulties. The child may not be able to coordinate swallowing efficiently. They may later prove to be messy eaters who spill things all the time or are especially inefficient in dressing themselves. Shoelaces could prove impossible.

Here are some other symptoms. Remember, this list is not exhaustive.

♦ Irritability and poor sleep patterns

♦ Poor writing and drawing ability

♦ Inability to stay still

♦ Short attention span

♦ Difficulty in carrying out instructions

♦ Frequently falling and bumping into things

♦ Too trusting, with little sense of danger

If I haven't got it now does it mean that I am safe?

No. It doesn't. It is possible to suffer from acquired dyspraxia, which occurs after damage to the brain. It could be the result of a stroke, an accident or a medical disaster. This usually happens to older people and the difference is that they have a memory of praxis that they will need to restore. Children with developmental dyspraxia don't have this lost or damaged memory to recover. For them the brain is, literally, immature.

What causes it?

It is not the result of poor physical strength. It is not a deformity. It does not show up under neurological examination. In spite of all the research in recent years and the raised profile that it has, the causes cannot be clearly identified. There may be an inherited tendency that predisposes members of a family to this and other conditions. There may have been a momentary problem – an illness, a lack of oxygen at a crucial stage of foetal development or at birth that caused damage or it could simply be that particular connections between cells are at fault. The fact that it can co-exist with other disorders like Dyslexia or Attention Deficit Disorder means that diagnosis can be difficult, since all the symptoms intermingle.

Who gets it?

The condition affects up to 4 per cent of the population but at least 70 per cent of those affected are male. Sufferers are generally of average or above average intelligence. Teachers can therefore assume that there is probably at least one child with the condition in every class. When you look at it in this way you can see that it is not something that can be easily dismissed. Of course, in specialist provision the incidence could well be over 50 per cent. Remember too, that only those children where the disorder seriously impairs learning or development are ever properly diagnosed. There are many others who are not recognized and instead are given other labels – like thick or slow or clumsy. If you start thinking of difficult boys in classes that you have met, you might be able to see some of the symptoms of dyspraxia in the behaviour they displayed. It is clear too that thinking about unpredictable developments within the structure and connections of the brain can also help you come to terms with the way some boys behave in lessons and around the school.

How is it diagnosed?

Occupational therapists, speech therapists, teachers, psychologists, educational psychologists or paediatricians can perform tests. But it is the parents of the child who usually carry out the most effective initial diagnosis. They will know that something is wrong. They may not realize what it is but they will know that something isn't right. They will have noticed difficulties and developmental surprises, perhaps from very early on in the child's life. A weak sucking reflex is often an early indicator. The child will appear healthy and alert and there might be no obvious explanation for the difficulties they are facing.

Dyspraxia may exist in isolation or as part of, or as a symptom of, another disorder which makes diagnosis difficult. Once other disorders have been excluded and dyspraxic signs and symptoms identified, then a diagnosis is usually possible. It is often the case, however, that a diagnosis is only made when a child starts school.

So what happens next?

When a child is diagnosed with dyspraxia they should at least be assessed by an educational psychologist with a view to a statement of special education needs being drawn up. Any subsequent Individual Education Plan (IEP) will help everyone. It will help teachers to respond to and plan for children who are often very talented. It might offer advice to parents about strategies and may suggest possible dietary supplements such as Evening Primrose oil and fish oils which some have found effective. The IEP will be essential in guaranteeing the dyspraxic the extra time in examinations that is their right. Achievement in examinations will have long-lasting consequences.

But most importantly, a statement will reassure the child that they are not alone. Their needs and frustrations have been recognized. There are things that will help. It will also reassure parents that their concerns are being taken seriously. There is another important point here too. There is a good chance that the child will proceed to further education. A statement has consequences for funding and might trigger important support for a family in terms of grants and equipment. This should be explored.

What is needed at an institutional level is that the condition is treated with sympathy and from a position of knowledge. There should, ideally, be someone in every school, at every level, who knows something about it and can offer some advice. It is not an isolated condition. There are sufferers in every school, possibly in most classes, and statementing procedures are a significant means by which the profile of understanding can be raised.

4

The Dyspraxic Child

The first thing to say is that there are no physical attributes that distinguishes them from anyone else. A dyspraxic child I know said, 'I am able bodied. I have full use of my arms and legs. I am not a freak. I am not confined to a wheelchair.' As Dr Amanda Kirby says (see Resources) 'It is a hidden handicap'. Even if we can't see it, dyspraxics do have a disability. Even if it is hidden from view it is still a real one.

They may find it difficult in building successful relationships within their own peer group. They can be perceived as odd because their thought processes are different, making their conversation strained. The connections that others see as a conversation builds are not recognized and what they say can seem irrelevant. They can seem out of sync with everyone else. Their behaviour can seem immature. The sort of relationships that boys establish, competitive and teasing, are hard for them to master since they are never sure which comments are real and which ones are jokes. When they eventually try to emulate the fundamental basis of male interaction they usually get it wrong. They are unable to decode the social environment quickly enough.

As a result the dyspraxic child is often a loner. He is often a boy who isn't very good at the things a boy

Dyspraxia

is supposed to be good at. He will be poor at sport. Even simple things like kicking and throwing can be challenging.

There are often problems with speech and the processes that underpin it. For a start, dyspraxia can affect the production of sounds because it can affect those muscles that control speech. The organization of language in the brain may be affected. So, poor sequencing skills may affect the order of letters in words or the order of words within a sentence. They could have difficulty in identifying the right sounds. Imitating sounds, whistling, blowing balloons could all be impossible. It is not a surprise that a diagnosis of dyspraxia is often made by speech therapists. Naturally enough if they can't relate a letter or combination of letters to the sound it produces, they will struggle to grasp spelling patterns.

Words are often troublesome. If the child cannot find the right words quickly enough in their heads, then their ability to tell a story or to recount an event may become confused or lengthy. If they cannot organize their thoughts they will struggle to establish an order. So there could be lots of repetition, hesitations, false starts. It will require a great deal of effort.

It wouldn't be unusual to find that the dyspraxic child can read very fluently and with insight and comprehension to themselves, but find it impossible to do so out loud. In the sensory area there could be symptoms too. The child might have a poor sense of touch – or even an over-developed one, which could mean that certain textures are very difficult to deal with, like, apparently, mashed potatoes. Some dyspraxic children find having their hair brushed or cut is very uncomfortable. The labels on clothes could cause extreme irritation. It will not be a surprise to learn that buttons and, especially, shoelaces can be impossible because of an inability to judge where body parts like fingers are at a particular moment.

They could also have problems in blocking out unwanted sounds in order to concentrate on a specific one. This perhaps provides a useful way of trying to understand what they face in their day-to-day lives. They are swamped by a flood of information that overwhelms them before they can process it. The ordinary world as we experience it shouts them down. They must focus on something that is slipping through their fingers and build a series of individual actions to achieve it.

When I run and kick a ball or when I am trying to hang a piece of wallpaper I don't have to work out every individual movement separately. The action comes as a package and I can concentrate on it without having to worry about the rest of my senses being overwhelmed. I can call upon the collection of remembered actions to perform the task and continue a conversation or listen to the radio at the same time. It happens all the time – writing, washing, chopping onions. There are things that we do every day that we take for granted that a dyspraxic child could find tremendously difficult – like stepping on and off an escalator.

Just think of the frustrations of being able to see instantly what you need to do but having always to persuade your muscles to catch up. A top-class cricketer has instant coordination between eye and hand. By the time the dyspraxic has worked anything out it is too late. It must feel as if you are at slow motion and the world is whizzing around you at double speed and swamping you before you are ready.

Dyspraxia

You can imagine that living with a dyspraxic can be very trying. Their frustrations can take a number of forms. They demand the sort of patience that comes from knowledge and understanding – and a teacher can be best placed to provide this. Families will need help in dealing with the misunderstandings of the ill-informed who will label their child as lazy or difficult.

♦ They will need reassurance and strategies.

♦ They will need to know that someone is interested and that they can put the difficulties they are facing as a family into a context.

♦ They will need to know that someone cares and recognizes the qualities of their child.

Family is very important to the dyspraxic child. It should provide security and happiness, a haven from a complex and confusing world. Sadly this isn't always the case – and difficulties can be magnified hugely if that security disappears with the collapse of a family.

A dyspraxic child can certainly create tensions within a family unit because they are so demanding. They will need extra attention and their parents can expect to act as intermediaries between them and the outside world in a more sustained way than they will with their other children. Other family members – as well as the child themselves – will need to understand the full implications of the condition. If it affects one child then the knock-on effects will impact on all family members. A dyspraxic child might in fact be happiest when at home. It is predictable, safe and controlled. This is quite a contrast with the behaviour that many other teenagers display, who try to distance themselves from their parents. It is something else that marks them out as different.

What is quite possible is that because the real world is so frustrating and depressing, the dyspraxic child will retreat from it. Perhaps into a fantasy world or into a world of endless plans. What will happen in the future, what they will do, what they will become. This focus on the future as a means of escape does not mean that they are ever likely to achieve it. It brings with it no practicalities or strategies to achieve goals or to realize plans. It is an imaginary world, peopled by imaginary friends, full of plans and schemes.

At examination time particularly it might be necessary to encourage them to focus upon the present. It is achievement now that could make their future attainable. Plans made need to be turned into reality – and the only way that will happen is through organization and planning – and, as we've noted, the dyspraxic child will need help to do this. Of course, in this they are no different from many of their peers. But with the dyspraxic it co-exists with so many other symptoms and difficulties.

The emotional immaturity that comes with dyspraxia can extend childhood well into the teenage years. They give you unconditional love and reliance.

They are emotionally fragile and can be easily hurt. A harsh or unkind word expressed in the heat of the moment can have a disproportionate effect.

Their interest and knowledge can be unexpected and astonishing. They can become almost obsessive about a topic or issue to the extent that it can dominate their lives. Yet they cannot always show sufficient concentration to achieve in a conventional sense in school. As a teacher it isn't long before you come to share their frustration. You know how intelligent they are, the talents that they have. Yet everything has to be accomplished through a thick veil of fog. They can see what they want to do. But it is too slippery. It is almost within their grasp – but not quite there. They have to nail the jelly to the wall. They know that they can't. You need to make sure that they keep on trying.

You need to keep in mind this idea of an unconventionally wired brain. The information or the knowledge of how to carry out a specific action is in there somewhere. It has just been stored in the wrong drawer. And you will never find your socks if you put them in your pants drawer. And perhaps this silly analogy can point us towards something sensible. You might be able to stop putting your socks in the wrong drawer if it is labelled. That is what dyspraxic children sometimes need. A bit of basic organization. Simple solutions. They might not be able to fasten shoelaces but does that matter? Buy elastic sided shoes or trainers. Why was Velcro invented? They will need other people around them to help them find such solutions.

If you stop to think about it, poor muscle coordination or inadequate signalling within the body could have some unpleasant consequences. Think of toilets and toileting. Any part of your life and procedures can be affected. There are many things that a teacher needs to know, for they will be the first port of call for anxious parents, especially for those working in the earlier years.

If you needed reminding, teaching is more than just a job. Teachers have the opportunity through their understanding and sympathy to influence lives in radical ways. Dyspraxics and their families need these things from you.

5

Behaviour

Some dyspraxic children negotiate school successfully.
Some do not.

For some, school is an inescapable confrontation
with inadequacy. They know they can't cope very well
– and they have to deal with this every day. It is not a
satisfactory experience but they are forced to repeat it,
seemingly without end. Behavioural issues can result.

Obviously they suffer from considerable internal
conflict because of the difference between what they
want to do and what they can achieve. Dealing with
other people is also very frustrating and their condition
can lead to real exclusion by their peers and a lack of
understanding from adults. If, for example, they have a
difficulty in following instructions, their request for
them to be repeated could mean that they are accused
of not listening. They can become frustrated and irri-
tated by such perceived intolerance. The inability to
concentrate can lead to similar unfortunate labelling.

The stress of being at school can lead to poor behaviour in response. Indeed some children can display
temper tantrums because the world seems deliberately to misunderstand their condition.

By the time they progress through secondary school
the result is likely to be that the student will decide to

opt out of school. This shouldn't be a surprise. If they feel that their needs are neither recognized nor met, they can feel isolated and forgotten and so eventually reject school. It is much easier to be a clown or to become a disaffected isolate in order to hide any limitations and avoid failure.

This is where the idea of dyspraxia being a 'hidden handicap' (Dr Amanda Kirby's words) starts to impact. Our society is ready to recognize needs for the physically disabled. Ramps and lifts are rightly provided for children in a wheelchair. No one would expect a deaf child to be able to sing in key or then follow that with a suggestion that all they need to do is to try harder. We would make sure that their needs were met and the necessary equipment made available.

Dyspraxic children are no different. Their condition needs to be recognized and a strategy developed to accommodate it. Emphasis needs to be placed upon success rather than failure. This is a common theme throughout this book – be positive. In this way, over time, you will thus make a contribution to dispersing the low self-esteem that develops among some dyspraxic children. You will also modify and improve behaviour. However, there might also be a pressing issue with the behaviour of others, for dyspraxic children are frequently the victims of bullying.

Bullying

What parents might soon come to realize is that the dyspraxic child appears to have the word 'Victim' painted on their forehead. There is no doubt that the issue of bullying will eventually come the way of the teacher.

Why should this happen? Why are dyspraxic children so frequently the victims of bullying?

The answer lies in the nature of their dyspraxia, its consequences and the way that the dyspraxic child is perceived.

We've said before that they are often hopeless at ball games. In the overall scheme of things this is hugely unimportant.

Except when you are a boy.

For it is on such a basis that you are judged and the skills of the dyspraxic child are certainly not going to enhance the success of the team. So they are not picked. And because they are excluded from a defining activity, they can become loners and thus isolated, easily picked on. The bullying will almost certainly begin in a verbal form as a response but it can soon take on physical expression.

However hopeless they might be, they can still see themselves as being just on the edge of becoming very good, for they know what they want to do. It's just that something gets in the way. Next time they will be fine. So they don't shut up about it. They keep putting themselves forward for the team. They crave acceptance. One more chance, just one more chance. The others will eventually get fed up.

It is quite likely that they'll be regarded as odd, simply because they don't fit stereotypes. It will often appear to their peers that they have not achieved the proper milestones. So their ability to look untidy, their hair, their posture, their walk, will all flash out signals. What they are just doesn't add up. Their written work can resemble a disaster; their work displayed can inspire derision. Yet their general knowledge can be exceptional. So they might be seen as freaks, any verbal facility resented. The dyspraxic's inability to control their emotions may lead to them being labelled as immature. This can be exacerbated by their obvious difficulties in basic areas like getting dressed, tying laces, eating.

The presence of verbal dyspraxia will make them less articulate or perhaps a little slower to express thoughts. It is also possible that they prefer playing with children who are either younger or older than themselves. Their own peers are the ones they avoid – and they are the ones who establish reputations. From here it is but a short step to bullying.

The dyspraxia might be the cause but the solutions and strategies are no different than they are in any other circumstances.

A school should establish clear-cut rules about how it should be dealt with. A support network needs to be provided and a mentoring scheme established. Remember a dyspraxic child will usually relate well to someone who is older.

Watch out for the obvious signs.

♦ The child walking alone in the playground.

♦ The child who is isolated on school visits.

♦ A shortage of Christmas cards.

♦ Not being invited to parties.

♦ Others being reluctant to sit by them.

♦ Bruises and scratches.

♦ Possessions disappearing.

♦ A sudden deterioration in the quality of work and in verbal responses.

You see, in the end what dyspraxic children are is that they are different. And sometimes the others in the pack will want to drive them out. It is also true to say that dyspraxic children are special, with a refreshing innocence and an engaging relationship with their work. Teachers will need to show vigilance if they are to be given the space in which to succeed.

The emotional consequences of dyspraxia do need careful consideration. The world they try to inhabit can be difficult enough. Their days can be stressful. They live with frustration, anxiety and failure. Their self-esteem can be low. They may have behaviour problems that these issues provoke. But the inconsistent development of the brain can affect their emotional development too. The information they get from their experiences and senses may be impaired, so they may not be able to understand their feelings. They may show inappropriate emotions, or too much. So a small set-back can become a disaster. They can be too easily moved to tears. They can focus obsessively upon events like birthdays or holidays, repeating plans and ideas constantly until they appear to be real. They may pursue the repetition of questions and their answers as they try to fix an issue in their minds. This means that ordinary life as we all learn to come to terms with it, can contain additional frustration and disappointment. These frustrations can make them seem immature and certainly emotionally fragile.

Without the consistent ability to read people and situations or to recognize accepted behaviour, friendships may be difficult to form. So on the one hand they want to keep up with their peers and to achieve but their behaviour will seem so odd. It is no surprise that they are frequently the victims of prolonged bullying. We mustn't let it happen.

There is undoubtedly a touching level of sadness in life with a dyspraxic. Whatever they want always seems just outside their grasp.

Managing change

They are not very good at it. The most stressful times for the dyspraxic are often the times of transition, when the child has to come to terms with major changes.

The times of change in anyone's life can be tricky periods to negotiate but for a child with dyspraxia they can be fraught with considerable danger. Just as one environment becomes familiar and can be negotiated carefully, allowances made, compensations established, things suddenly change radically. Familiarity is replaced by uncertainty. These are key occasions when parents should be especially aware and supportive and new teachers watchful. There needs to be careful communication. Change needs to be managed by an institution and by individuals. The right people need to know the right things. It is one of those things that teachers need to do – to find out about the new children they are about to inherit and so know about any issues from the start.

Sadly, however much we may say otherwise, schools are not always effective when it comes to passing things on. So parents have every right to nag and pester if it makes sure that the job gets done. After all, can they rely upon anyone else ever having their child's interests truly at heart?

6

Assessment and Diagnosis

You start off by asking yourself why. Why bother? What is the point? You can't cure it. But that would be wrong. Assessment is important. If a child is assessed as having dyspraxia then they are labelled. That labelling process can be a defining moment. It can trigger support and funding. With a label there comes an action plan. Suddenly parents can be reassured that the problem has been identified, that it will be taken seriously and that consequently something will be done. You can find things out and you can make things better.

This is, sadly, not always the case. One problem is that diagnosis isn't straightforward. One professional will say one thing and another might say the opposite. There isn't a unified set of symptoms that can trigger a diagnosis. It is a diagnosis arrived at through the consideration of a number of factors. There is no one test or screening process that can identify the condition conclusively.

So what might a professional be looking for? The basic criterion would be motor coordination that is significantly below the level expected on the basis of age and intelligence. This can be assessed by standardized tests.

Questions should be asked. How does the child interact with their environment? Is there a discrepancy between what happens and what you would normally expect? Any difficulties should have been present since early development and there will probably have been significant delays in achieving particular developmental milestones.

Difficulties seen by parents could be confirmed by any one of a range of specialists, including speech therapists and physiotherapists, but generally in school an educational psychologist will probably make the diagnosis. They will need to look at the history of the child's problems and determine whether verbal skills are greater than physical skills to a significant degree.

The range and nature of the specific assessment tools used currently in the identification of dyspraxia lie outside the scope of this book. Tests are developed all the time. What is more important is that teachers should record any concerns they might have and pass them on to the educational psychologist. Particularly useful are observations on the child's behaviour during play. A great deal can be learned from this. In addition, has poor posture been noted? Are there difficulties in eye-hand coordination?

Obviously the involvement of parents is vital, for they can provide an insight into the child's skills in daily life. Their observations are usually found to be honest and realistic. After all, they want the best for their child and are aware that something isn't quite right. The educational psychologist will contribute to the preparation of a statement of special educational needs. This document will clarify the roles of everyone involved and spell out the nature of their responsibilities and obligations. It can also offer guidance to parents, areas to explore, who to contact, what to read. We all need to realize however that there is no quick fix, no magic bullet. A statement will establish what the problem is and what it is not. It will focus resources. But it won't offer a cure.

The best sort of assessment would involve both health services and education. It would examine the whole child, drawing together all the relevant information. It is logical to assume that coordination difficulties may lead to psychological problems and to poor motivation, concentration and then to social difficulties. So the whole picture is important, not just the separate symptoms.

The label that comes from the assessment will ensure that the difficulty is taken seriously. It is not that this is a new condition: far from it. It is more that it is now being recognized. The label will bring responsibility and focus. It will also bring people together who have similar problems that can have so many benefits for everyone concerned. And it will, through the sharing of experience, allow people to adopt a more positive view. The diagnosis will concentrate on the things the child can't do. What you have to do as a teacher is to emphasize to parents and to the child what they can do.

There can be no doubt that dyspraxia should be considered as a priority for resources, even within restricted budgets. Problems can be long term and they can be intrusive. A sufferer can display poor social skills, low self-esteem, learning difficulties and behaviour problems. Even if you put on one side such concepts as responsibility and obligation, if no attempt is made to address these issues then the future call on resources could be far greater. Dyspraxia is recognized as a disability within the criteria established by the World Health Organization – there is an inability to carry out an activity within the range considered as normal. We need, as professionals, to respond to this and ensure the best for the children in our care.

7

How to Teach a Child with Dyspraxia

There is no big secret, no special formula. Good teaching that is structured and focused works for dyspraxic children just as much as it does for everyone else. So be sure to stick to your principles and you won't go far wrong. But of course there are particular features of dyspraxia that you need to note carefully. These may help to explain the ways in which a dyspraxic child can respond. Before we examine the specific issues that a child might present at the different stages of their school career, there are some general points that we need to consider.

It will certainly help if you do your research and familiarize yourself with the condition. You will achieve a deeper understanding and you will be better placed to discuss the child with parents and offer informed advice. A well-informed teacher, especially in the early years, can provide a great deal of assistance. By reading this book you have already shown a willingness to enhance your knowledge and to be sensitive to their needs. Many of the difficulties you encounter with an individual child will make more sense if you have a context in which to put the information. With this understanding, you can work out the best way of teaching the child and maximizing achievement.

Dyspraxia

In the frantic activity that makes up a normal day in school it is all too easy to forget what you really should remember. All too easily you can find yourself condemning a dyspraxic child for things that they have no control over. If they forget things then it isn't always their fault. An inability to recall stored information is a difficulty in the processes of storing rather than of memory and is certainly not a sign of laziness. Remember how those messages are being re-routed along twisting suburban lines behind a slow engine. The child probably wants to learn things just as much as the next but for them learning takes 20 times the normal effort. This is the case whether the child has to learn where the pencils are kept or where the toilets are or whether they are trying to remember the details of Thomas Hardy's poetry. In fact any information learned may not be reliably recalled. It could get lost in transit for neurological reasons as we have seen, an idea suddenly shunted into weedy sidings away from the main line. The child shouldn't be blamed for this.

♦ First of all, any teacher needs to ensure that instructions are broken down and simplified. It is important to maintain eye contact when giving instructions to an individual dyspraxic child. This will help them to concentrate.

♦ Explain things in a simple uncomplicated way. Make sure your instructions remain constant and unchanged.

♦ Remember, almost everything can be broken down into a staged process with a logical sequence. It is one of the things that teachers are good at – and all children in a class can benefit from this approach, whether dyspraxic or not.

♦ In these circumstances patience is a virtue. Be prepared to repeat yourself calmly and frequently.

♦ With younger children particularly, it can be helpful to repeat things gently, leading and prompting the memory until previous learning can be recalled. Just as music can prompt forgotten ideas and experiences in all of us, so the memory can be prompted through a rhythmical, phonological approach to issues such as reading, writing and maths. Sing or chant or clap – but link it to a particular concept.

♦ Ensure that you communicate your expectations clearly and concisely. Ask questions to ensure they know what to do. Ask them to repeat the task to you before they begin.

♦ Offer encouragement and keep reminding the class of the task and the sequence.

♦ It is always helpful to establish a predictable routine and firm guidelines. Sudden changes in routine can cause major problems for a child with dyspraxia.

♦ Simplify choices. We are all surrounded by too many choices that we don't need. A dyspraxic child is perhaps less able to deal with them than most. In these circumstances choice doesn't bring freedom. It brings confusion. So why offer six different essay titles? Is anyone really disadvantaged if they only have two?

♦ Ensure that the child knows where they are in the overall shape of the lesson and how much time they have left. Give them clear time checks, make sure there is a clock visible; 'There are ten minutes to go, so start bringing this section to a close'. This is a very important technique to acquire for examinations.

♦ A dyspraxic child might need additional time to complete a task satisfactorily.

♦ Stay alert to the child's needs. They may find it difficult to wait for adult attention, so be ready to seize the moment. Get on the train before it pulls out of the station.

♦ Try to minimize distractions. A child with dyspraxia may be very distractable so a simplified classroom will help. Keep screens and boards free of unnecessary information as an aid to concentration. This will encourage focus.

♦ Sitting at the front will help concentration by reducing intrusive distractions.

♦ Remember that they are emotionally fragile. They might be unable to deal with disapproval or criticism within the context intended. A careless or casual word could provoke a disproportionate response. Try to stay calm – and learn to manage your own feelings of guilt when an unguarded word leaves them devastated.

As a teacher you will know that reading, writing and Maths all require a great deal of planning and organization. It is possible therefore that the real nature of any difficulties may not show up properly until the demands of the classroom become more structured.

Then you will see a child who is unable to retain learning consistently. You will see the disruption caused by problems such as handwriting, reading and following instructions. All this may obscure the child's intellectual potential.

What is most frustrating is the inconsistency that comes with dyspraxia. What you know today you may not know tomorrow. The plan needed to perform a task could disappear suddenly.

They may become less articulate when excited or upset. Long stories or explanations can't be sustained and there might be constant repetitions of statements and questions as the child fights to maintain concentration and fix information in their head.

And from many of these issues there is no escape.

Taking a dyspraxic child away from school on a visit could be especially challenging for a teacher, who would have to confront all the difficulties normally contained within the family. Residential experiences are today increasingly popular at all levels. In these circumstances it would be wise to establish a dialogue with parents at an early stage. Exchange visits where the child stays with the family of another student overseas can be quite stressful. However, as long as the placements are chosen properly and the hosts fully informed, there is no reason why they should be excluded from the benefits that there are in living abroad with another family.

We can start now to look at the different stages of schooling. A lot of the advice here is transferable from one stage to another. A child's requirements don't necessarily change when they move from one school to another. So it may be that ideas that can help are outside the age range of particular concern. A child at any age could still have all the problems presented by a pre-school child with little or no improvement. The emphasis throughout must be on good teaching that supports children and their learning.

8

Dyspraxia in the Pre-school and Nursery

All teachers – at whatever stage – can make a great deal of difference to the development of dyspraxic children through their understanding and patience and through a commitment to preserving and boosting self-esteem. Where teachers of the pre-school child are especially valuable, in nurseries and playgroups for example, is in giving support to parents who may be coming to terms with a recent diagnosis or, more likely, trying to understand why their lovely child is somehow different. Teachers of this age group need to have readily available practical strategies for support, both for children and their parents.

You really will be in the front line in managing the condition and the parents. In playgroup or nursery, as with all children, vital foundations are laid. For better and for worse. If basic skills are not successfully established, then everything in the future could be compromised. Problems that become obviously apparent later on are first seen here to a greater or lesser extent.

An observant teacher or professional might look at a child and begin to form a picture. They will be slowly accumulating evidence. They should register concerns when they see a child

- who is less inclined to participate in play

- who is perhaps less active

- who avoids large play equipment

- who is more passive, more anxious.

Their reputation may already start to coalesce as that of an outsider, slightly beyond the fringe of interaction and activity. At this stage they are not usually labelled or ostracized. Children at this stage will generally accept others for what they are, but the process of isolation may have started. Dyspraxics learn very quickly that there are things they find harder to do than others and even at this young age they will not want to be different from their friends.

- Some dyspraxic children are hypersensitive to certain stimuli. They might have an aversion to bright lights or loud noises. You can notice this on occasions like Bonfire Night or at Christmas time. Such an aversion could become discernible if the child is involved in a play or a performance, especially when they are older. They could be very uncomfortable under bright lights. This will become the old story for dyspraxics. Wanting to be involved in something and their body stopping it from happening.

- There could be an oversensitivity to certain textures like the labels on clothes or to wool. They could take particular objection to hair combing or nail cutting.

- The child may seem accident prone, more clumsy than most, lacking in basic coordination.

- They may look awkward when running, walking or even standing still. Can they actually stand still? And how do they stand? With feet splayed out? Can they stand on one leg? All these things are significant features to watch out for.

- They could be very messy or untidy eaters. They could in fact have difficulty in coordinating the sequence of chewing then swallowing.

- They could be slow in learning new games and their rules.

- A skill mastered today can be forgotten tomorrow.

- They might have no concept at all of position – such as behind, in front, on, etc.

- You may find that they have an astonishing memory in one particular area. They may be able, for example, to identify any make of car they see with uncanny accuracy from a minimum of information. However they may have a poor memory for things that they hear.

- Making choices could be extremely difficult.

- They might not be able to follow simple instructions in the correct sequence.

The child could be having problems making sense of a world that seems to be flying past at high speed, never slowing down long enough for them to get a grip on things. The child will realize very quickly that there are things they find harder to do than others. At any age they do not like being different from their peers.

For parents too it can be a difficult time. They will want the best for their child and may sense that something is not quite right. If a diagnosis has not yet been made then they may acquire a reputation as being over-anxious parents. This could certainly affect the way that they are seen by a school. Professionals should always ask themselves why parents have concerns. Are they legitimate? Are they justified? You need to listen to their observations because they know far more about their own child than anyone else. Never dismiss them out of hand.

It could have been a very frustrating time for parents, trying to convince a doctor that something is wrong. It is not unknown for parents to be seen as fussy or troublesome. They might need someone to take their concerns seriously and to listen. It is a very important time, for it might be when the first interventions and strategies begin. Parents might need you to reassure them that their child's problems with the labels on clothes is not too alarming or indeed unique. Parents will want to know the answers to many questions and they will also want to find out what they can do to make things better for the child that they love.

A simple series of graded exercises to be carried out either at school or in the home could be proposed. An example could be walking between two lines about a foot apart. This will help coordination and could be part of a game for everyone, not just a child with dyspraxic tendencies. Then you could move on to riding a scooter between the lines. This can take on a more imaginative dimension if this path is imagined as the route to a special place or the route to a reward.

But of course the most important question they will have is whether their child will ever grow out of their dyspraxia. Your professional responsibility is to be honest. They will probably not. What might happen though is that over time they will adapt their behaviour to accommodate the difficulties they have. They will learn to live with them and to manage them, if they get the right help. Once an awareness of their difficulties is raised then proper interventions may begin.

9

Dyspraxia in the Primary School

Arriving in primary school is a serious moment of change. The familiarity of home is replaced by the uncertainties of school. There are new unfamiliar people; there is new furniture to bump into. It can be a very unsettling experience. A well-informed and sensitive teacher can make a big difference. Teachers should never underestimate the importance of their job, and in this section we will look at the influence the teacher can have and the strategies that can be adopted to support the dyspraxic children in their care. The child may have managed to avoid certain activities in playgroup or nursery as a way of hiding their difficulties. However, now that the curriculum becomes more structured and formal they will have to confront their problems. They will have to deal with large amounts of new and confusing information and more specific physical demands. Certainly the gaps between children will widen – and conclusions will be drawn about those who can't carry out particular activities with confidence – catching a ball, dressing, eating and other domestic tasks.

The child may have significant issues to face – like using the toilet efficiently, managing clothing, playing with other children, adjusting to a classroom. After all, it is a busy and noisy place, in the middle of which the dyspraxic child is supposed to sit still. They may, for example, find themselves sitting with their back to the teacher for part of a lesson. They will have to maintain attention while dodging backwards and forward to follow the focus of the topic. This could be very difficult. The move to the primary school could be a very tiring time, for the school day will be longer, with different rules and requirements.

A teacher may quickly form the impression that a child has significant levels of immaturity in a number of areas – for example in writing and drawing. What may trouble them most of all could be an inability to concentrate that will definitely have an impact on attainment. But a teacher isn't powerless. Always remember, there are things that you can do.

At home, the family manages problem situations. But in primary school the same activities need to be managed alone – like getting changed or putting a coat on – for the child will be spending a significant time away from their parents.

This is an important point, and before we look at learning issues in the classroom, a primary teacher will have to consider a number of significant domestic issues so that the real business of school can take place. In order to do this, teachers and other classroom workers need to have an understanding of issues so that they can go on to offer advice and solutions to parents.

♦ Parents seeking advice could be advised to label clothes clearly.

♦ They should look for Velcro fastenings on shoes (I mean, who else was it invented for if it wasn't invented for dyspraxics?).

- Elasticated waists on shorts and trousers can be helpful.

- PE kit could be worn under normal school clothing in order to minimize difficulties.

- Personal hygiene could be a problem. An electric toothbrush will help to sort out one area at least.

- A sensitive teacher will also watch closely and lend discreet assistance when necessary, to other children as well as dyspraxics, in order to minimize embarrassment.

- Eating in school could be a real problem. Cutlery may still be difficult to master and a child could become particularly self-conscious. So perhaps sandwiches are a better practical alternative.

- Suggest that parents provide drinks that don't need pouring. Boxes of juice with a straw are a simple solution.

I am afraid to say that if we have problems getting the food in at one end then we can have just as many getting it out at the other. The child may not leave themselves enough time to get to the toilet. They may not recognize the signals soon enough so that by the time they get there they might be in a bit of a rush. If you add on the tricky business of getting trousers up and down then you will see that the potential for accidents is extensive.

The processes involved in wiping the bottom might be difficult to coordinate. So the opportunities for embarrassment are huge. One of the results can be constipation. You might want to discuss with parents the idea of establishing a regular toileting regime. Going to the toilet at the same time every day, perhaps before school, could definitely help. Elasticated waistbands should be recommended and the school should have a ready supply of wet wipes. The routine involved in visiting the toilet should be reinforced at regular intervals and emphasis placed upon hygiene. The whole class will benefit from this anyway.

There are other symptoms of control that will have an impact on learning. The obvious factors that will hinder achievement in school are problems with coordination and manipulation. There are, however, things that a teacher can do. You don't have to accept things as they are. You can do things that really will make things better. And, as small improvements add together through repeated practice, then gradually significant progress will be noted.

What the teacher can do to help

Writing

A dyspraxic child may not have developed an appropriate tripod grip for writing. Their grip might weaken quickly or they may apply too much pressure in order to maintain control. Handwriting can thus appear uneven and crude. It might not be possible to write along a line or to keep words separate. Letter formation might not be consistent. Writing at the top of the page could be better than that at the bottom.

♦ Experiment and try to find a pen that the child finds easy to hold. There are lots of pens around these days – with foam grips or with textured barrels, for example. Triangular shaped pens are sometimes a successful solution.

♦ If written work is sometimes too untidy then allow the use of a pencil. Mistakes can be easily erased and the finished product will look more acceptable to the child.

♦ Of course a computer can help to make work presentable, indistinguishable from the work of anyone else. Computer skills are important for the future anyway.

♦ A child still needs to acquire some facility in handwriting. However difficult it is, it can't be replaced entirely. Repetitive exercises on letter formation can be employed as a means of slowly improving handwriting. But writing out a favourite poem or piece from a story can be more fun.

Music

Music has an important part to play. It stresses a sense of order and sequence. The consequences of disorder are instantly apparent. However, learning to play the recorder, that integral part of the primary experience, can be difficult if you haven't got reliable fine control of the fingers. Perhaps the drums would be a better alternative. Songs and word games like 'I went to market' can be very useful as a way of teaching memory and sequence.

Scissors

These might be very hard to use. Holding the paper in one hand and then making the correct open and close movements could be almost impossible. Spring assisted scissors could reduce coordination difficulties. Starting with firmer paper could help. Cutting squares or rectangles from a long strip is a way of developing skills.

Rulers and other equipment

Using a ruler can be awkward since it requires the child to hold it down with one hand and to draw with the other. A metal 'Safety Ruler' with a groove stamped into it, or one with a raised handle or ridge might help. Make handles for smaller pieces of mathematical equipment with lumps of Blu-tack. A compass is another tool that is difficult to master. A blob of Blu-tack into which the point can be placed aids stability and accuracy.

Manipulation

Lego can help manipulation. Building with bricks helps planning and sequencing. Hand exercises or the making of shapes with clay or plasticine can warm up the muscles before activities such as writing begin. Screwing loose plastic nuts and bolts together is another obvious activity that helps coordination.

Sequencing

When you consider how the brain might be having difficulty remembering certain actions, it will be no surprise to learn that sequencing could be a problem. You can help by using picture stories and asking the child to put them in the right order.

Classroom management

♦ One of the most important things that a primary teacher can do to help is to make sure that the dyspraxic child sits facing the teacher as much as possible. Maintaining eye contact can be an important aid to concentration. The teacher should ensure work is presented in short steps or stages and that the child is asked to repeat the instructions given to reinforce understanding. It will sometimes be useful to use worksheets and exercises allowing for short and structured responses in order to reduce the amount of handwriting required.

♦ Select grouping arrangements with care. And naturally don't label the dyspraxic child as slow just because their writing is weak. They have other valuable intellectual strengths that mean they can contribute in an effective way in group situations. This can be an important way of improving self-esteem and the way they are seen by their peers.

♦ Remember, group work can build bridges between children if the groups are selected sensitively.

♦ Classroom support assistants can achieve a great deal with dyspraxic children if they are deployed effectively. They can work on particular exercises targeted to make a positive impact. You will always find that they enjoy individual attention and can thrive in situations where they are not competing with their peers. Additional adults in the classroom can help the busy teacher achieve these sorts of objectives that would otherwise be very difficult to schedule.

Dyspraxia

♦ The observant teacher will see other problems however, that will be a cause for particular concern. Social skills might be poor and interaction with others clumsy or uncertain. In many ways this might trouble parents much more than anything else at this stage. They will begin to fear what the future might hold for a child who is finding making and maintaining relationships a serious challenge.

It should be quite clear by now that a dyspraxic child lives with lots of frustrations. And sometimes that frustration boils over. It shouldn't be a surprise. The child may suddenly become aggressive or disruptive or far too easily moved to tears. There may be a real sense of anger because the child will want to do better but is aware that something intangible is interfering with achievement. It is also very possible that the child is a victim of bullying. As a boy he will be regarded as immature, not quite right. He will be excluded from games and spend a lot of time on his own. He will walk round the edge of the playground rather than be active in the middle. He may seek the company of either younger children or of adults who will accept him more readily. It doesn't take long for a reputation to be formed within the peer group. Suddenly they are someone who isn't quite the same as everyone else. And to a child at this stage, conformity is everything. And as friendships form and coalesce, suddenly a child can become a loner, generally because of the things they can't do. These issues are explored in more detail in a chapter of their own.

You may observe these things. It is important that you share your observations with colleagues and other professionals and with parents. They will probably be very pleased that someone can confirm their own doubts and concerns. This might indeed be the first stage of more formal assessments. You can also refer parents to relevant publications (see Resources) which could be very reassuring and productive.

All children find primary school very tiring. For the child with dyspraxia the problems are magnified. Completing simple actions will require even greater concentration and focus. A teacher needs to be aware that quieter periods of relaxation are vital if they are to help the child manage the amount of information that is in danger of swamping them on a daily basis.

Of course as the child progresses through the school their ability to deal with different situations will improve, of course it will. A dyspraxic child isn't fixed forever within an unresponsive body. They do change, they do develop naturally, though perhaps at a slower rate. The remedial exercises suggested should eventually have an impact. So the child will change, their confidence in some situations will improve, their concentration and focus will develop. It is just a longer process.

Primary school teaching does become more formal and separated into different subjects with different requirements. It is all part of the inevitable process that feeds through into the timetabled structure of secondary school. This formality often brings with it greater assessment, both internal and external.

Teachers need to have the statementing process well in place by this stage. This might guarantee the child who is pressured for time due to organizational issues, more space in which to show their real abilities.

This won't be appropriate for all dyspraxics, but where, in the teacher's estimation it will be helpful, children need to be encouraged to accept that there is no shame in taking extra time. They are entitled to it.

Homework

This is a big issue. Schools at all levels pride themselves on their wide-ranging homework policy. It is a means by which they promote themselves. They ask others to make judgements about them on the basis of homework. They like to think that it shows they are a no-nonsense institution devoted to learning and academic achievement. Whether this is accurate or not, homework does give the dyspraxic child some difficulties.

For a start they may have to concentrate and work much harder than the other pupils in the class. This means they may be very tired by the time they get home. At this point they are expected to do more of what they found difficult in the first place. It is a difficult issue – because they don't want to be singled out by not doing it. At the same time, though, they could feel totally overwhelmed.

Their greatest need is for organization, and both home and school can help here.

♦ A homework diary needs to be kept.

♦ A prominently displayed planner at home and in the classroom can help by indicating regular tasks and deadlines.

♦ The use of kitchen timers and stopwatches can be used to counteract poor time awareness.

♦ Tasks can be planned and the amount of time they need could be predicted.

♦ Tasks can be simplified and broken down into small achievable stages.

All it needs is a little thought and understanding. Lots of others in the class will benefit from this too.

Home-school links

A positive relationship between home and school will benefit the child enormously. It is the way that the greatest progress will be made. Everyone working together can give the child joined-up support and focus. It will definitely help parents deal with a condition that they might not understand and appears to have been visited upon the family out of the blue. It will also bring information back to school that can help in assessment and in targeting support. Something that is especially important in a condition like dyspraxia, which is not widely recognized, is that parents are reassured. Their child's problems are not of their making. It hasn't emerged because of their poor parenting skills. And as we have seen, you can show them that there are practical solutions that will help.

10

Dyspraxia in the Secondary School

This is an awkward time for all children, for it is a time of change, and change can be unsettling. The difficulties however are magnified for a child with dyspraxia. The secondary school is a transitional phase, a move into early adulthood. The agenda might change but the problem reduces itself to one simple fact.

The dyspraxic child can appear to be left behind, stranded in earlier years.

They may not have mastered fastening laces, for example. A simple and relatively unimportant skill in these days of elastic-sided shoes. But it can assume huge symbolic significance – as a task that most of us carry out without thinking and yet one that they can never really get hold of. A representation of their failure. And if their primary school experience has been unsatisfactory they may have low self-esteem.

The whole purpose of this book is to set a positive agenda and to show how the condition can be managed and how a child with it can achieve. But it has to be acknowledged that the child might have struggled through primary school. The condition might not have been managed and they may not have been treated with sympathy. It is quite possible that they feel rejected by the education process if it has never addressed their needs. The frustration that is felt may well be displayed in poor and disruptive behaviour. It is a very complicated time.

The difficulties of transition

The whole experience of moving to secondary school seems designed to be deliberately confusing. Instead of a small, contained area, the learning environment can be a sprawling mass. Going to school involves moving around almost randomly, in response to an arbitrary timetable of lessons. Their first experience of secondary school could be of a seething mass of older pupils, all knowing where they were going, so unlike the simpler world of the primary school. The registration group will be full of children they do not know. Personal space will not be constant. There will more than one table or desk where learning can take place. We want our schools to be interesting and challenging places. The richer the environment the better the school. Yet that also means the more opportunities for disaster for a dyspraxic child.

And then there are all those teachers. It would not be unusual if they were meeting male teachers for the first time. Some of these teachers may not have any understanding of, or sympathy for, the condition. They may deal rather harshly with a child they regard as lazy or obstructive. Then there might suddenly be a supply teacher covering for a teacher. Or there will be a teacher who doesn't teach the class very often – say once a week – and so the gap between lessons can make the work all too confusing and all too forgettable. Different faces, different rooms, different tolerances, different expectations.

Many children find this difficult but settle into their new environment in a week or two. But the child with dyspraxia will take much longer. They may feel disorientated and get lost, arriving late to lessons. It will take them much longer to internalize a map and to pattern their movements round the school. If they are separated from the others in their class who they have been following all day, then they could become completely disorientated. Teachers they don't know will shout at them for being in the wrong place when they don't even know where the right place is.

They may be taught in bigger groups that may mean more noise. This increases the chances of being distracted in class. And of course, as the youngest in the school they have no status at all.

Preparations

It is vital that careful preparations are made by both parents and school prior to the arrival of children with dyspraxia. All children will benefit from effective liaison, but none more so than those who might be experiencing difficulties.

It is still possible, though increasingly unlikely, that dyspraxia will not have been diagnosed by the time the child starts in secondary school. Generally the secondary school will receive information from the primary school. This information must be distributed so that all staff are aware. Unguarded comments resulting from lack of information can be embarrassing and hurtful.

So proper liaison provides a bridge between primary and secondary and is designed to ensure there is a continuum linking the two phases. It should ensure that the earlier good experiences are built upon and the bad ones are not inadvertently repeated. Information needs to be passed on and the child needs to know that this has happened. It is reassurance, that in a way their old teachers are still watching over them. Dyspraxic children are no different in this than any other. They all have their stories to tell and the secondary school experience will be a better one if we listen properly across the key stages.

If the child is to manage the change to secondary school with some success, then the process needs to begin before they even arrive. What the dyspraxic child needs is familiarity, a gradual introduction to this new phase in their life. It might be difficult for a primary school to do this but early visits to the school are crucial, both as part of the class and as an individual. Familiarity is important so perhaps a support worker can accompany them around the school. Dyspraxics, more than most, will need to be prepared for the movement and the sea of faces. Introductions could be made, both to teachers and to other workers in the school. Of course, the teachers are quite likely to forget over the summer holidays but it is important for the child that these connections have been made. It makes it all seem just a little more familiar. This is an opportunity to find all the important places – the office, the dining hall, the toilets – without the distractions of others.

This process could represent a sense of handing over. Perhaps the support assistant from the primary school could introduce the dyspraxic child to the support assistant in the secondary school. The idea of a familiar and sympathetic face who can act as a point of contact is a very useful one. What is clear is that, in all of this, correctly and imaginatively deployed support workers, well-trained and properly informed, can make a huge difference. They could provide something fixed in the ever-changing day of our secondary school.

A lot depends upon the sort of induction programme that has been established and how Learning Advice Departments and SENCOs operate. It might be that significant staff will have already visited their partner schools to find things out and to meet significant pupils. This sort of practise blurs the boundaries between the two phases and so makes transition more manageable.

The child needs a plan of the site and the parents need to display it prominently at home. It won't stop problems happening, because we all know that maps are different from reality, but it will develop some familiarity.

Parents can be involved by encouraging them to rehearse the preparations for school and the route to be followed. The summer holiday is a good time to practise going to school!

The emotional minefield

Adolescence can be a difficult time for anyone. The dyspraxic may encounter additional problems. They will still experience difficulties with physical tasks, sequencing, organization and perception. Handwriting might still be laborious and untidy, though the use of a computer will minimize problems in this area.

One of the important issues that emerge in the adolescent years is body image. Because physical exercise can prove so problematic a dyspraxic child might avoid it completely. The danger is then that they could become quite unfit. So it is important that they find an activity with which they are comfortable, Swimming is a possibility that is worth exploring since the water will support the body while the relevant movements are arranged and organized. Olympic qualification may not be possible but it is a healthy activity that can help the development of effective coordination.

All dyspraxic adolescents will be delighted to learn that computer gaming can make a genuine contribution to an improvement in hand-eye coordination. 'I am not wasting time. I am in therapy.' How convenient. A very useful or irritating excuse for extended sessions in front of a computer screen, depending on your perspective.

Of increasing prominence will be emotional difficulties. The child will recently have been one of the oldest in the primary school. This brings with it a certain status. They are expected to set an example and to help the teachers they now know very well and who obviously know them. They will also have been able to mix with the younger pupils in the school, playing with them in an unthreatening environment. The move to secondary school represents an immediate transition from oldest to youngest with a consequent and immediate loss of status. Almost overnight there is no one to play with. Suddenly all their social weaknesses can be exposed. Their failure to keep up with their peers will mark them out as odd.

There are not just the usual adolescent issues. The dyspraxic child may have retreated into their own fantasy world, fuelled by the very computer games that could be helping their coordination. The computer and the games console draws them into a controlled and limited world where they can live out lives freed from their frustrations and where, if you make a mistake, you can just start again. They can take risks and model different responses to situations safely. When the outside world is so complex they may just try to avoid it, both emotionally and physically. An inability to ride a bike, for example, could mean that they would stay close to home. Not for them the easy freedom of the streets.

They may not be sociable with any success and so will neither be popular nor cool. They will be outside the mainstream. An uncertainty in relationships with their peers can mean that they are not sure how genuine others are. So isolation and loneliness can be inevitable. What becomes important then is the family and the security of home. Which in turn emphasizes the differences between themselves and their peers, who all like to pretend that they want to break away.

This inability to read others can make male adolescence very confusing, since male relationships are often built around teasing and criticism and if you can't judge your interventions in fast-moving conversation well, it is going to leave you stranded. The lack of success for a chosen football team can have a devastating effect. The comments of your peers about a defeat are not about the team; they are about you. It is a very complicated thing to disentangle. In two important areas – in sport and in teenage conversation – they are likely to be significant underachievers. In these circumstances a boy hasn't much hope.

Is it all bad news?

Well no. There are advantages of course in arriving in a secondary school. It would not have been unusual for a dyspraxic to be the only identified child in their class. On arrival in secondary school, with a larger population drawn from a range of schools, the child will find that they are not alone. A support group can be established, bringing children together. This can be particularly useful for parents who can be reassured that they are not alone. They can exchange strategies and advice. The school can take the initiative through the SENCO and bring parents together.

This will also serve to raise the profile of dyspraxia among the rest of the teaching staff of the school. They may then see common features in the children within the group, lending the condition credibility in those areas where it is needed. Children too will feel less isolated, less alone – and will know more faces around the school as a result.

School transport

This is an important subject that schools will need to consider for those dyspraxic children coming to school in Year 7 particularly. Obviously they will need to know where to catch the bus and how to manage either their bus pass or their fare. But the company needs to be advised that the child needs to sit close to adult supervision. Furthermore it is unlikely that they'll be able to stand for any length of time. If the transport company are aware of this then it will help to ease understandable parental worries. An older brother or sister or a neighbour could also keep a discreet eye on things. Teachers would be well placed to find a reliable guide who travels on the same route. This kind of 'buddy' support is extremely effective in many different areas, not just on the buses.

Sharing the knowledge

The SENCO and the Learning Advice Department should act as a repository of knowledge on dyspraxia and other conditions. They should be able to offer advice and workable strategies across the range of subjects that a secondary school teaches. Staff need to be aware that a child with dyspraxia could well be of above average intelligence but with poor achievement. They can also provide something that is equally important – a base and a haven for all dyspraxic children in the school. If a school can actually establish a physical location for such a base – and it may support children with other difficulties too – then it will help to ameliorate the initial difficulties of transition.

I think the idea of such a support system is worth exploring because it gives a sense of importance. You might find school difficult and the other pupils may not be very sympathetic but we value you, who you are and what you can do. It is a base, a stable haven in a constantly changing world. It could be just a place to eat sandwiches. But they will always know that it's there. Classroom assistants, working from this area can then help to disseminate knowledge to subject staff and provide continuity. It can also be a place where they can go when the going gets tough.

Obviously the use of support workers in the classroom is something that needs to be addressed as a whole-school issue. But in the case of dyspraxia, teachers need to be aware that additional adults in a classroom can make an immediate impact. They can mediate between the child and the task, repeating instructions, guiding and structuring. Remember, they will always respond to individual attention.

The importance of the form teacher

The early years of the secondary school could well be the most difficult for the dyspraxic child. The problems they have will start to have a greater impact, especially socially. They will have to contend with cruelty and unkindness. Their relationships with their classmates could be difficult. Everything about the school could be disorientating. As a result they will rely a great deal upon relationships with their teachers. The two most important people in the school at this time are likely to be the SENCO and the form teacher. The former probably helps most to manage the condition. The latter helps to manage the child. Perhaps this is too simplistic but it does indicate the real importance of the role of the form teacher.

A form teacher or mentor will need to keep in close contact with parents throughout the secondary school career in order to maximize support. They can give advice about what can be done at home to parents who might be anxious for their child. A form teacher will find useful advice in the Primary School section of this book that they can share. The advice there still pertains, even if the child is a little older, because there is no easy or quick resolution to some of these problems.

Offering advice is what much of teaching is about, usually about academic issues. Teachers know what books to read, what questions to ask. When you start advising on dyspraxia you start to talk about domestic things too and lifestyle issues. Don't be embarrassed about this. It is practical advice that parents will need.

They will need to think about things like appropriate and manageable shoes for a child who can't fasten laces and about tricky issues like ties. For example, the form teacher can make sure that there are plenty of copies of the class timetable available, both in school and at home – on the back of the bedroom door, on the fridge, in the school bag. This can be reinforced in school every day. The child can be reminded of what lessons they have and where they should go. They can be reminded of the names of the teachers they will see and they can be asked to repeat them.

Does the child have a watch? Do they use it? This is an important part of negotiating the examinations that will come to dominate their school experience. They will need practice in wearing one. Many children with dyspraxia have a poor concept of time and they need to make an early start in developing a relationship with it. They need to understand time values – how one period of time is longer than another. Your advice should suggest the use of a digital watch, which is easier to read. They also have alarms that can be set to give instant reminders and help to achieve short-term objectives. You can help in the classroom by providing an egg timer. A simple device but it is visual and a child can see how much time they have got left. This will also help to develop a sense of time values.

Dyspraxia

Often what the dyspraxic child needs is time – and they deserve it. Discuss events, encourage them to read newspapers and to watch the news. This will give a structure for conversation and improve their self-esteem.

Don't forget that teachers who don't know much about dyspraxia can actually make things worse. They can label the child as slow or untidy. They can criticise, they can insist on work being repeated. They might even impose a detention or some other sanction, which will merely be a punishment for having a condition. So they might need someone who understands and who can intervene on their behalf. Staff will notice that the child may do badly in lessons but significantly better in one-to-one situations. They will relate well to the attention they receive. It allows them to focus without the distractions of peers with whom they have difficulty forming relationships anyway. If teachers know what the reasons are, they will respond and make allowances.

As a form teacher you need to focus on successes and give out positive messages about improvement and success. You need to promote a feel-good attitude. As a support to the child your comments are crucial. They need to feel that they have a haven in the fast-moving complicated world of school.

So focus on the positive. What have you learned today? Tell me one good thing that happened to you yesterday. The dyspraxic child might not always want to respond. They might not wish to be positive. But you must do it. You must try to shift the focus to good things. What else can you do?

You can hold regular meetings where the child can be given an opportunity to catch up on their work. This would be a particularly productive use of lunchtime, for a dyspraxic child will often spend this period avoiding things. So this sort of space in the day can be really useful, whether provided by the SENCO or the form teacher. And if LSA support can be provided then so much the better. A flexible interpretation of working hours could provide important support. They will need a moment or two to understand what happened in the morning and get ready for the afternoon. Other things can come out of such a group – an understanding of a pupil's interests and a means of exploiting them, for example.

Of course as they get older then this time can be used very profitably to complete coursework assignments because they might need a little more time to present things successfully. Ensure access to a computer for use at this time.

One thing to remember is that time is made available in the primary school for the development of basic skills like handwriting. In secondary school there is often no time set aside for these things. The assumption is made that they have been acquired. What the school requires is speed and legibility. A form teacher can find the time needed perhaps in registration or at breaktime to practise handwriting. However important word processors have become they have yet to replace handwriting completely. It doesn't have to be repetitive exercises in letter formation. It could be the copying out of an important piece of text or an interesting news item. They will find an enthusiasm and an interest. Good support from a form teacher will help them explore it.

You need to remember this idea of dyspraxia being a hidden handicap. Even though you can't see it, it doesn't go away. The support offered must be sustained, just as it would be for a child with a more visible disadvantage.

Other subjects

Each subject that is taught in a secondary school has its own arena and its own rules. This means that they have their own particular and perhaps unexpected difficulties. In **Science**, for example, the seating available in a laboratory could make life very difficult for a child with poor balance. They could be concentrating so much on maintaining their balance that they have no idea what is going on in the lesson. Perhaps it would be better for them to stand during any experiments. Indeed in some experiments, particularly in the early years, they could be a positive danger. So it might be better to let them watch rather than expose them to danger and ridicule. Someone – the SENCO or the form teacher – needs to take the initiative and tell the Science department in order to pre-empt problems. This emphasizes the key point about supporting children with any sort of difficulty – the need for effective and professional communication between schools to begin with and then between departments.

Drama is a subject that could help enormously. The bright lights of the stage might be too uncomfortable but the opportunity to work behind the scenes in productions or to be involved in improvisation in lessons will help to raise self-esteem.

The importance of **Physical Education** lessons is such that they merit a chapter all to themselves. Dyspraxics need good well-structured opportunities to develop confidence and maintain a level of fitness.

What the form teacher needs to watch is that they are neither mocked nor bullied because they can't run very well. Of course they are quite capable of making things worse for themselves. They might want to be involved in things everyone else says they can't do. In their head they can play football, or netball, or cricket well enough. On the pitch their colleagues don't agree. So they might keep putting their name forward for the class team and keep being rejected. This is not something in which a teacher should interfere and you certainly shouldn't insist that the child is part of a competitive team. Any defeat, rightly or wrongly, will be blamed on them. This will clearly make things worse. What you should do is find alternatives where they can help and where they can succeed – in environmental clubs, for example, or in the school magazine or website.

English has significant emotional content, particularly in the study of literature, and can provide an opportunity for the expression of personal feeling and for empathy with characters and situations. It is important to encourage an examination of the feelings of others in the controlled environment that a book provides. **Design and Technology** on the other hand is fraught with difficulty, where inadequate control and manipulation could place us on the cusp of disaster. The idea of a dyspraxic child with a sharp knife in one hand and a slippery onion in the other can send shivers down your spine.

In **Maths** they may find it hard to line up columns of figures in order to do calculations. So make sure that they have access to squared paper which will stop figures becoming transposed. Remember that any activity involving scissors could prove exceedingly difficult to perform with any accuracy or precision.

Get organized

A carefully arranged strategy to the school day will help enormously and a teacher can help to establish a successful one. The daily business of school needs to be resolved. Without a careful and thoughtful approach the whole day can become a mess. Of course the child needs to begin to take some responsibility for these things because this is the way that they will need to approach the rest of their lives.

♦ A transparent pencil case is very useful since it provides a quick and easy check that everything is in place. They are also insisted upon by examination boards as the only cases permitted in the exam room. So start early.

♦ Encourage the child to have a place for everything and to put things back properly so that they can be easily found.

♦ Encourage the making of lists of things to do that are then regularly reviewed.

♦ Post-it notes are very useful. They can provide instant temporary reminders and can be displayed prominently and in a variety of places.

♦ Encourage them to join groups and school societies.

This sort of underpinning will allow them to function both in school and beyond. To see a role model like a teacher giving this sort of advice is very influential.

Making choices

With increasing maturity students will become more involved in their own learning and eventually be in a position where they can make choices about what they are going to study. When they do reach this stage they may well experience a sense of considerable relief. They will be able to put behind them those subjects which have caused them difficulty or embarrassment, like Physical Education or Art.

But these choices have to be made carefully. They could be intellectually drawn to reflective subjects which might actually be harder for them, like History. Here the pressure to produce substantial pieces of written work in a pressured examination performance could bring its own problems. A dyspraxic's disadvantages may preclude them from successful involvement in practical subjects but it doesn't necessarily mean that they will be good at others instead.

An important factor could be that the student may be more comfortable working on their own, at their own pace. So they could perform well in project work. Looking for a subject that gives such opportunities could be profitable.

Every child is individual and so it's impossible to make any broad or definitive judgements and recommend particular subjects. But it does seem to me that Information Technology could be a good choice, since the computer does even things out so that the playing field is, as they say, a little more level and it will always play an important part in a dyspraxic's school career. Certainly, there is no need, in most circumstances, to make any exemptions from the normal school curriculum for dyspraxics. Work with it, or work around it. Don't give in to it.

Work experience

This can be a moment of great significance in the secondary school career. Suddenly the emphasis is upon looking forward towards a future of employment rather than upon daily concerns. It is a time to try out possibilities and to have new, more adult, experiences. It is, though, a change and changes bring with them the anxiety of the unfamiliar. Responsibilities for the dyspraxic student might, for the first time, involve managing transport and money for daily expenses. It is a first tentative step into an adult world. Obviously the hosts need to be fully briefed by the school so that they will know what to expect. It would be wise to ensure that they are aware of any limitations on the student's performance to avoid embarrassment and misunderstanding. The student would suffer considerable distress if they were asked to do something that they couldn't perform because of their dyspraxia. So the placement needs to be chosen with care.

An initial visit by the student with a teacher would be helpful. It would also be advisable to give them an opportunity to rehearse any journey that may be unfamiliar before the start of the placement. The location of toilets should be established. Lunch arrangements need to be clarified. A teacher shouldn't forget that it is the basic domestic issues that must be sorted out before a learning experience can happen.

11

Dyspraxia and the PE Teacher

The main reason why Physical Education should have a chapter all to itself in this book is because it is such a nightmare area for the dyspraxic child. It could prove to be one of the most stressful areas of their day. Unless they are treated sympathetically and – dare I say – professionally, their sense of self-worth and their world-view could be damaged forever.

PE teachers sometimes see themselves as poor relations, overlooked and marginal figures. Here they have an opportunity to play a central role. Dyspraxia is a condition that has a particular physical manifestation. Sympathetic PE teaching is vital to the overall success of the dyspraxic child. It can have an enormous impact.

Every PE teacher will have seen an undiagnosed dyspraxic child at some point. The boy who stands there and waits for the cricket ball to hit them before they raise the bat. The girl who is not sure which direction to run in rounders. The child who appears to run as though wearing diving boots.

Other children around them will be achievers. They will have an instinctive grasp of the skills they need to play games. The hand-eye coordination, the spatial awareness. The dyspraxic child will stand out. Certainly ungainly, possibly inept. Their inability will have inevitable consequences. In team games they will be the last to be picked. In the changing room they may well be the first to be picked on. Given the physical nature of the lesson it can become the ideal area for intimidation and bullying. A pecking order is soon established and an inability in physical things quickly pushes you to the bottom of it.

Boys make judgements about each other often on the basis of their ability in games. Their status can come from their ability to emulate sporting heroes. The dyspraxic boy hasn't a hope.

What they do not need is ignoring, for this will only confirm prejudices and lead inevitably to the bullying to which a dyspraxic child is prone. A particular concern would be the changing rooms where careful supervision is needed to prevent intimidation and humiliation.

The issues are there for all to see in primary school and they just won't go away. There is the pressure to get dressed and undressed properly and quickly. There will be huge pressure to keep up with the rest of the class. At home there isn't much of a problem because Mum or Dad can help. But such problems can persist into secondary school. If laces become involved then everything can fall apart very quickly, and in a public arena. They will be instantly exposed.

The activities involved in the lesson can be very difficult and stressful. Ball skills may be non-existent. Climbing onto benches and apparatus can be daunting. The PE lesson can hang over them like a black cloud. A constant and public reminder of their inabilities. Dealing with the impatience of others in team situations will haunt them throughout the week. Their differences will be accentuated and their feelings of inadequacy reinforced by the hurtful comments of their peers.

So it is important that they are not humiliated in physical activity. They need encouragement and PE staff, who are clearly achievers themselves, can do a great deal to ensure the preservation of self-esteem. Their successes need praising and they need the attention and respect of the teacher. As role models for others, teachers always have a particular responsibility. So let's have a look at possible strategies that could be employed.

♦ A dyspraxic child will find kicking a ball very difficult. They will be unable to direct it accurately and will struggle to make judgements about how hard the ball needs to be kicked. Skills can be improved by using a large foam ball to show direction and the amount of force required.

♦ The child may be unable to stand on one leg and may be extremely inefficient when running. Trampolining can help balance, and swimming can aid coordination and sequencing. This should eventually have some impact on running.

♦ PE can do a great deal to improve handwriting through the use of directional games, reinforcing the concept of left to right movement. It will also help with the concept of order and direction. Movement to music will also help by giving a structure to movement and so help with the rhythm required for efficient handwriting.

♦ The teacher should try to develop a positive attitude towards Physical Education by offering encouragement and attention. Given the difficulties they face, there is the real danger that the dyspraxic child could become extremely unfit, with inevitable consequences to their long-term health. They might spend the rest of their life avoiding physical activity as a result of scars unwittingly acquired. Exercise is vital for their future well-being.

♦ The child will know that they are not as good as others so they don't need white lies about how good they are. They will know they are being patronized. They need realism. So the focus should be upon how they have improved upon past performance.

♦ The best sorts of instructions are simple ones. Don't issue too many in one go. Break down any physical actions into simple steps. Remember too that they may have difficulty in absorbing the rules for any new game. Keep those as simple as you can.

♦ Make sure that the child can hear and see instructions clearly. Make sure they are at the front and not peering at you from the back. They will find it extremely hard to maintain concentration if they are. You might find it helpful to ask the child to repeat the instructions to the class as a whole, to remind both them and themselves. This will also grant small but important status.

♦ Obviously don't ask dyspraxics to provide a physical example of an activity. This could further undermine already fragile self-esteem.

♦ Consider the use of different activities for dyspraxic children as warm-up exercises. The more fun and interesting they are, the more other children will want to join in. This is a good way of breaking down barriers. In a secondary school it might even be something as simple as using beanbags. They are often better than balls.

♦ Offer a more imaginative range of activities – pilates, yoga, Tai Chi could all help posture.

♦ Be aware that some children with dyspraxia might have poor posture and be unable to sit unsupported. Sitting cross-legged on the floor could be impossible for them.

♦ Try to minimize situations in which the child is chosen last when compiling teams. Many of us without dyspraxia remember the shame of being the one who no one wanted in their team. Now imagine what it must be like to be regularly humiliated in this way. But they mustn't be excluded. Appropriate involvement in team games will impact upon status and social skills.

What must not be forgotten is that properly structured and thoughtful physical activities can make a huge impact on the development of gross motor function. But motivation might be a problem. Why should they humiliate themselves in front of others? What purpose does it serve? The child might need to be encouraged to take part and to put their apprehensions to one side. To do this they will need to feel secure and valued. But activities like crawling and skipping can lead to measurable improvement. Swimming has been found to be especially beneficial. There are simple things that can mean so much and can lead to a real improvement in the condition and in the way the child is seen by himself and by others. This is the challenge that the dyspraxic child presents to all PE teachers, whatever age range they teach.

12

Examinations

Formal assessment plays a huge part in education. We have oral assessment, coursework and we have examinations.

These are the ways in which we register judgements about a child's abilities and we draw conclusions from them. Examinations are extremely influential, determining jobs, careers, education. Indeed, our whole system of education is built upon examinations. They are the focal point for most of the teaching that any child receives. So a school – all schools – must have in place strategies that help dyspraxics achieve results that confirm their abilities rather than reveal their dyspraxia. We know about that anyway.

There are three distinct phases to education as far as examinations are concerned. You need to put the information in. That is the teacher's job. The information has to be stored. That is the job of the student. Then it all has to be churned out at the right time and under pressure. You can see the problem here. Dyspraxic children can struggle with all three different areas. But the student's responsibility to store and then retrieve the information is a significant area of weakness.

The student who wants to succeed and feels positive because of the support they have received in school, will be best placed to achieve in examinations.

The dyspraxic child will need help to organize and to plan. This has to be a central message in everything to do with dyspraxics. They have difficulty in doing this so teachers need to get involved and help them to do it. After all, the secret to examination success at any age lies in careful preparations.

♦ Create a timetable and a study programme in the run-up to the examinations.

♦ Subject teachers should provide an overview of topics studied as a reminder. Identify key points or ideas that could act as a trigger for more detailed information.

♦ Shorter intense periods will be more productive than longer more diffuse sessions of revision for a student who finds concentration difficult.

♦ Encourage the use of highlighters to bring colour to the body of notes that has to be learned. Colours can be used to identify themes or issues.

♦ Use internet resources to add variety and visual interest to revision.

Coursework is always going to play to the strengths of the dyspraxic student, especially in the age of computers. They should be encouraged to achieve the highest marks possible in this element, which will compensate for any slight underachievement in time determined situations.

A teacher can help a great deal by providing a structure – a framework – for any coursework. Many people find it very difficult if they are presented with a blank sheet of paper. They need a framework, a way of breaking down a longer piece of work into smaller manageable sections. Smaller objectives leading to something more significant. It would be important to start early on in the course. Explain the requirements and get parents involved if you can. They might want to help with field trips, for example. There is no reason why they shouldn't go along, if appropriate, to support their child. This would then enable parents to repeat the field trip at a later date if necessary. As we have noticed all along, we are not talking about particular strategies for dyspraxics alone. This is just good teaching.

There needs to be a programme of study skills that will show students how to learn. They might need to relate knowledge to visual clues by designing word maps or spider diagrams. You can make tapes of revision material that can be played on a personal stereo. Everything needs to be designed to develop confidence and to make material familiar and internalized.

Fundamentally, what you must do as a teacher is to help the student manage all the information that is thrown at them on a daily basis. You need to help them filter it and process it. You need to help bring order to the chaos.

Once you have developed the techniques required to help the dyspraxic student learn and revise, you need to help them structure their approach in the examination room.

A response to pressure is a very individual thing. Some people thrive in examinations, enjoying the focus and purpose it gives to the work they have done. Others feel overwhelmed by the experience.

Dyspraxia

The dyspraxic child is likely to need support if their self-confidence is low as a result of the frustrations of their education. They could approach examinations with foreboding. The examinations will be difficult; there are no two ways about that. The nature of examinations does not play to their strengths – the pressure to work quickly, to plan and organize, are precisely the things they have always needed help with. They may find it hard to deal with their own anxiety. They may find it hard to recall information in the correct order. They may struggle to write quickly and legibly.

What they will need is a strategy for approaching the examination experience. Teachers should have plenty of advice to offer, since in many ways examinations are what their job is about.

Individual training sessions could be very useful. Tutorials and individual meetings will help dyspraxics to concentrate and to plan their revision. Ensure they have a revision plan and schedule written in diary form. 'Monday 5.00pm – 6.00pm History. 7.00pm – 8.00pm Maths.' That sort of thing.

♦ Break down revision into manageable chunks.

♦ Propose a plan to negotiate the written paper. Indicate in which order questions should be attempted.

♦ Focus on how to use the available time. Specify how long should be spent on particular questions.

♦ Try to ensure that someone is there at the start of the examination just to offer reassurance and to calm apprehensive students, A familiar face, telling everyone that the examination is fine, no problem, can be important for all candidates.

- A check can also be made that the necessary equipment has been brought.

- There is no reason why you shouldn't write the time plan out and display it at the front of the examination room for the benefit of everyone. So you could write '10.10am start question two. 10.35am start question three.' Tell the dyspraxic student when the examination has reached these points, or adapt the advice for them if they are entitled to extra time in which to complete their answers.

- If appropriate, provide dyspraxic candidates with a separate room so that they will not be distracted by others and will have more success in maintaining fragile concentration.

It is likely that any statement of educational needs will indicate that the dyspraxic child can have additional time in examinations. For some this will be no help since all it will do is to prolong the agony. However, for others it may allow them to flourish. You need to reassure the student that there is no shame in accepting this allowance. Many children are reluctant to take the time, even if they are entitled to it. They feel embarrassed, singled out. Different, when all their school career they have tried to be the same. But if it is their entitlement then they should have it. Teachers will need to speak to dyspraxic students at an early stage about this and perhaps involve parents. It might be wise to consider taking 'mock' or preparatory examinations without any additional time allowance to assess how the student performs when writing under time pressures. This will provide evidence for any discussion that might be needed. Then, if extra time is felt to be useful then give them an opportunity to practise with this concession in internal exams. It is not really something that should be sprung upon them when they arrive at the real SATS or GCSE examinations.

13

Education Beyond 18

Like many young people, the dyspraxic student might view college and university with a sense of liberation. Finally they will be able to put behind them all the frustrations and forget the things that reminded them of their inadequacies and concentrate on what they can do. They can make choices about what to do and how to do it. Some will be all too eager to leave school, where they have always confronted failure. But they need to be encouraged to think carefully. They shouldn't reject education too soon. It is important to arrest any sort of decline that can lead to frustration and anti-social behaviour. There are, for example, higher levels of dyslexia in the prison population, with huge ongoing costs to society, and there is every reason to assume that the position is much the same with dyspraxia. So it is important that everyone gives off encouraging messages.

Incidents of bullying should by now be in decline. There is less of a requirement to conform, as teenage lifestyle fractures into a whole host of possibilities. In the early part of secondary school everyone had to be the same. Now everyone wants to be different.

But of course it is never so straightforward. Choices bring stressful interludes and the move towards greater independence can be haphazard. But leaving school is another change and it can be managed with help in the same way other transitions are managed. Knowledge and preparations are the keys.

Support will be needed in filling in application forms and in preparing CVs but this is normally offered to all students anyway. Once again there must be an emphasis upon the transfer of information. The form teacher, who has, we hope, established a working relationship over a number of years, needs to feel confident someone else will be stepping into their role.

Naturally this transition brings with it issues about self support. All parents fret about this but with dyspraxic students there are added concerns and important decisions to discuss.

♦ Is the student ready to leave home and deal with a new way of life?

♦ Is the student ready to deal with a new environment, with the need to form new relationships with students and tutors?

♦ Would the student benefit more from studying in their home town rather than moving away?

♦ Or should the emphasis be upon somewhere that is easily accessible?

These are big decisions and an informed teacher can make a helpful contribution to the debate. A particular issue that could be explored is whether grants and allowances are available for students with dyspraxia. A lot depends upon what their statement said. Teachers should consult their LEA and the DfES for the current position. It may be that Disabled Student Allowances would be available. These are not means tested and are grants, not loans, so they don't have to be repaid. The financial implications of this can be quite significant. It might also be helpful to contact individual institutions to see what they can do.

Even if financial assistance isn't forthcoming, other levels of support can be accessed, particularly with regard to assessment procedures (examinations, coursework, dissertations, that sort of thing) and technical support (laptop computers). So it is definitely worth doing. It is another example of how communicating information can be so important.

All those stages that were required when the transfer was made between primary and secondary all those years ago need to be replayed, with the intention of developing familiarity with a new environment and the demands that it will make. The issues may be slightly different, that's all.

Does the student have a timetable for changing and washing clothes?

Is the student ready to start managing money?

Does the student have a filing system for storing notes so that they can be easily retrieved?

All those things for which they previously relied upon others for help will become pressing issues when they become their responsibility.

Schools will also need to prepare for interviews, especially for the dyspraxic child who is not socially adept. It is inevitable that the inability to recognize facial expressions in a conversation or interview, the inability to maintain good eye contact or the shambling walk and slumped body shape, the weak handshake, will all give an impression that the student is not sociable and immediately inaccurate conclusions maybe drawn. Naturally, their clumsiness, their failure to pick up on clues in a conversation, will be less of a problem if the prospective institution has been made aware of the condition and know to some extent what to expect.

It is an exciting time for everyone, and brings with it worry as well as opportunity. With careful and sensitive planning it can be managed successfully.

14

Into Adult Life

This book is designed to inform teachers to ensure that they are best placed to deal with the dyspraxic children that they meet. Thus strategies for adult sufferers fall outside its remit. However, teachers will want to know what will happen to the children with whom they have built close relationships during school years. After all, teachers are preparing their students for the complexities of adult life, both within academic study and beyond. They will want to be in a position to offer practical help and guidance. It is what teaching is about. They will be expected to speak with the authority they have always shown and their views will be respected. That is why teachers want – need – to be informed. This could be the great unspoken fear of parents. What sort of future can they expect?

Well, the condition does not go away. It continues into adult life. But it is certainly possible to adapt to its features. There will be some measurable improvements as sufferers mature. There could indeed be a maturation of parts of the central nervous system. The most important thing that happens however is that the dyspraxic finds ways of dealing with the condition. When you are at school, school things seem to be important. When you are older the inability to kick a ball is largely irrelevant. So they learn to operate successfully within the parameters that the condition has established. They adapt their lives, limit their expectations. Perhaps in the end we all do this. All of us have to deal with very complex lives. We accept it and we establish a routine to manage it. A dyspraxic adult needs longer to establish a schedule but in needing a carefully arranged routine they are no different from the rest of us.

Recent technological energies have been centred upon making our lives easier. So we have dishwashers, automatic cars, electric carving knives, computers, all designed to even out the differences between us. A carefully managed home environment will ensure an effective lifestyle. They might need some initial support in learning how to manage money. DIY and cooking could prove problematic but there are approaches and adaptations that can be employed which are preferable to complete avoidance. It might take them longer to develop independent living skills but they will happen.

The focus must be upon establishing supportive relationships and satisfying employment. Jobs requiring some sort of manual dexterity wouldn't be feasible but there are plenty of other opportunities. Lives so far spent in dealing with emotions and relationships mean that dyspraxics are sometimes drawn towards caring professions. When you consider their legendary handwriting problems, it should not be a surprise to learn that lots of doctors believe that they have been undiagnosed dyspraxics.

There will be things that they will be very good at. They might have acquired good verbal ability or advanced computer skills. The fact that they have always needed to be very organized could mean that they can flourish in a structured environment like an organization or a bureaucracy.

Their aspirations need to be linked to their intelligence rather than their past experiences in school. Careers advice that is informed and has an understanding of the condition and the student's needs is paramount, especially if the steps into adult life are to be made.

The baleful influence of dyspraxia shouldn't be dismissed lightly. Dyspraxia can lead to periods of depression because a lack of self-esteem may have become well established. Problems in establishing relationships could lead to loneliness and withdrawal. Adult dyspraxics can be prone to anxiety, nicotine dependence or alcohol abuse. Sadly, specialist treatment may be required.

As a teacher you need to try to counteract these risks by remaining positive and focusing on success and achievement rather than dwelling upon the things that can't be done. It is hard but you must be positive and upbeat. Without this the student will have no clear idea of where their strengths lie. We all need to take the responsibility to ensure that they leave school with a belief that they have a future to look forward to in which they can succeed.

15

A Cure?

There isn't one.

Developmental dyspraxia is not an illness or disease from which you can recover. It is a neurological disorder that you must cope with.

But there are thousands of adults with dyspraxia who have learned to compensate and to deal with their problems. Children diagnosed with the condition need to know this. The earlier a child is treated then the greater the chance of developing coping strategies.

All you can do is to teach the child praxis – to help them form ideas, to plan actions and to carry them out. There is no substitute for repetition and reinforcement. Some of this support might need to be specialist support. Speech and language therapists will help the child to gain control over speech muscles so that controlled and organized sounds can be produced. They would look at the shapes the lips adopt and where the tongue is placed. They will then help with the sequencing of movements. It is a slow process but improvements can and will be noted. But there is much too that a classroom teacher can do in all sectors, from pre-school right through to adolescence. Fine motor skills can be encouraged through play with toys such as puzzles and blocks in the nursery and through computer-based activities in the secondary school.

Individual help from a teacher or a learning support assistant could be very important in Maths or reading or spelling. This sort of attention from an adult will be much valued by a child who might find relationships with their peers hard to form. Always remember that dyspraxics can learn, dyspraxics can improve, dyspraxics can achieve.

While the basic repetition of tasks will help, much in the end comes back to individual attention. Without it they could become frustrated and unhappy adults, becoming a permanent drain on a society's welfare and prison systems.

Research does indicate that dietary supplements can have a beneficial effect. The suggestion is that learning and behaviour can be improved by the addition of highly unsaturated fatty acids to the diet, especially the essential fatty acid Omega 3. Evening Primrose oil tablets and cod liver oil are all said to reduce dyspraxic difficulties. Indeed trials in Durham indicate that an increase in fatty acids led to improved brain function in almost 40 per cent of the children involved. In fact, some improvements in areas like reading and concentration were quite dramatic. These supplements are readily available commercially and it is a development we should all keep an eye on. But no. At the moment we can't cure it. But in a way that doesn't matter.

What we can do as teachers is to convince children with the condition that they can achieve worthwhile goals. Yes they have a problem but it is not insurmountable. With informed understanding and proper consistent support, schools can make a real impact upon children with this unfortunate disability. And if our profession chooses to deal with it properly then it will make better teachers of us all and our schools will be more successful places.

Children with dyspraxia are delightful and caring people who deserve our support as they wrestle to grasp the slippery eel of coordination. They have, through no fault of their own, an unfortunate set of connections in their brain. They don't need to be condemned. Indeed who knows what sort of insights these different connections might one day bring?

They need structure and order; they need support in planning and in organizing. They need reassurance and security. If we are to provide the help they need and deserve, then we have to show sympathy and understanding. If their brains are not the same as ours then what does that matter? Who can say what is normal? Indeed if normal means average then who wants to be average? The dyspraxic child is different and those differences need to be celebrated.

The key to everything is sensitive and informed teaching. If you have read this book you have shown that these are the qualities you want to display.

Your pupils are lucky and are well on the way to getting the expert teaching they deserve.

Good luck.

Resources

The two names to look out for are Madeleine Portwood and Amanda Kirby. They have done a huge amount of work to develop research into dyspraxia and to develop strategies to help children with it.

Understanding Developmental Dyspraxia: A Textbook for Students and Professionals (Taylor & Francis; ISBN 1-85346-574-7) by Madeleine Portwood

Developmental Dyspraxia – Identification and Intervention: A Manual for Parents and Professionals (David Fulton; ISBN 1-85346-573-9) by Madeleine Portwood

Guide to Dyspraxia and Developmental Coordination Disorders (Taylor & Francis; ISBN 1-85346-913-0) by Amanda Kirby and Sharon Drew

Dyspraxia. The Hidden Handicap (Souvenir Press; ISBN 0-285-63512-3) by Amanda Kirby

Other useful books are *Helping Children with Dyspraxia* by Maureen Boon (Jessica Kingsley Publishers; 1-85302-881-9) and *Inclusion for Children with Dyspraxia/DCD. A Handbook for Teachers* by Kate Ripley (Taylor & Francis; ISBN 1-85346-762-6)